MW01277091

101

Quick Passing Patterns

Stan Zweifel
Robert Leboeuf

COACHES
CHOICE™

©2005 Coaches Choice. All rights reserved. Printed in the United States.
No part of this book may be reproduced, stored in a retrieval system, or transmitted, in any form or by any means, electronic, mechanical, photocopying, recording, or otherwise, without the prior permission of Coaches Choice.

ISBN: 1-58518-919-7
Library of Congress Control Number: 2004116741
Cover design: Jeanne Hamilton
Book layout: Jeanne Hamilton
Front cover photo: Ronald Martinez/Getty Images

Coaches Choice
P.O. Box 1828
Monterey, CA 93942
www.coacheschoice.com

Dedication

This book is dedicated to my daughter, Shannon. I have learned from you the ability to compete and persist. May all your dreams come true!

—SZ

This book is dedicated to all the players and coaches by whom I have been blessed to have the opportunity to work with and befriend.

—RL

Acknowledgments

Thanks to all my players over the past 30 years. It has been my honor and privilege to coach each of you.

—SZ

Thank you to all the staff members—past and present—at Muskego High for helping me stay on the right track. Special thanks to Stan Zweifel for being a great teacher and coach and always taking the time to help coaches like myself in our profession.

—RL

Preface

This book was written with the goal of developing a single reference on the quick passing game that coaches at all competitive levels would find useful. Our writing efforts are a by-product of 30 years of coaching experience with this particular offense. In reality, modern-day defenses, with their attacking type of mentality, have put a higher premium on protection and on routes that can be thrown on rhythm and tempo. As such, the need for a book such as *101 Quick Passing Plays* has never been greater.

The quick passing routes presented in this book are routes that can be employed against any defense and any coverage. They are simple to teach, yet flexible to use versus any coverage a team might encounter. Furthermore, these plays represent quick passing concepts that can be applied in a variety of offensive schemes.

The 101 plays featured in this book are organized by the type of pattern into which the primary route falls. Collectively, the plays cover a wide variety of quick passing patterns that can fit into a multitude of offensive schemes. While no one would advocate using all of these plays in any one game, every coach is encouraged to identify those specific plays that fit into his team's particular offensive system and the defensive scheme his team is going to face on a given week and incorporate them into his team's attack.

Each description of the 101 plays in this book includes the specific route that is run by each receiver, as well as any special guidelines for the quarterback. In addition, the play's description includes the pass protection call for the offensive line.

Hopefully, coaches will be able to use the plays presented in this book as building blocks of a successful quick passing game. The book was written for all coaches, regardless of their experience. If coaches gain from the book's contents, then the effort to write it will have been more than worthwhile.

—Stan and Rob

Contents

Glossary

40 FAST	A swing route to the halfback
40 M	A bubble screen to the third inside receiver
40 UP	The outside receiver fakes blocking the most dangerous man (MDM) and runs a vertical route
41 TURN	A 3-receiver route, with the receiver most inside running a 5-yard turn away from defensive leverage
41 UP	An out-and-up by an outside receiver
42 UP	The receiver fakes a hitch route and runs a vertical route
44 SHORT	A route where an outside receiver comes inside
44 UP	A flat-and-up route by an inside receiver; also commonly referred to as a wheel route
ARROW ROUTE	A route by an inside receiver where he releases outside at 45 degrees to a depth of five yards
BUBBLE ROUTE	A route where the receiver loses ground from the line of scrimmage and keeps his shoulders square
DART	The receiver gains width and verticality, looking for the ball over his inside shoulder
DOUBLE	Both the inside and outside receiver run the same route
FADE STOP	A route that combines a fade and a hitch
HITCH ROUTE	A route where the receiver pushes upfield to the outside shoulder of the defender. He takes three steps, then stops, and turns his shoulder to the quarterback.
LIZ	Motion to the left
M.D.M.	Most dangerous man concept; block the man in the best position to make the tackle

RETURN MOTION	The outside receiver starts towards the center of the field and returns towards his original alignment
RIP	Motion to the right
SLANT ROUTE	A route where the receiver works vertical for three steps and then breaks in at an angle determined by the coverage
SLANT VERTICAL ROUTE	A route that is designed to appear to be just a slant. The receiver, however, runs the route three steps vertical and then two steps inside. The receiver then makes another vertical slant to either the inside or outside, depending on the defender's coverage.
SMASH ROUTE	A route involving two receivers that is designed to attack a cover 2 scheme. One receiver takes a route in the flat, while another runs his route in the deep outside third over the flat route.
SQUIRT ROUTE	The inside receiver fakes a quick-out, which he then converts to a vertical
SWITCH	The inside receiver switches his route with the outside receiver
T-IN	The route looks like a quick-out stem, but the receiver comes back under coverage
UNDER ROUTE	A route where the receiver runs a shallow crossing route beneath the route of another receiver
WHIP ROUTE	The receiver runs a quick-out and stem and comes back in

40 Bubble Screen Package

Concept: A bubble route by the inside receiver to get outside leverage on the perimeter of the defense

Quarterback drop timing: Three steps

Key thoughts: The outside receiver or receivers should block the most dangerous man (MDM); they must read the leverage of the flat, curl, or flat-curl defender.

Play #:

1.   Queen Left Twins 40 Bubble
2.   Trips Left 40 M Bubble
3.   Trips Left 40 Z Bubble
4.   Trey Right 40 M Bubble
5.   Doubles Right 40 Bubble

Play #1—Queen Left Twins 40 Bubble

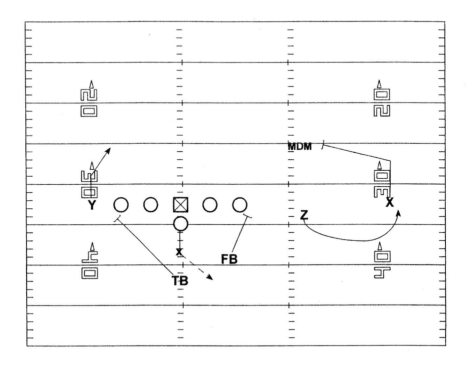

O-Line	Ram call
Y	Run a slant route
Z	Run a bubble route
X	Block MDM
TB	Block the C-gap opposite the line protection call
FB	Block the edge to his side
QB	Take a 3-step drop; drift to the side of the throw to cover in case of a fumble

Play #2—Trips Left 40 M Bubble

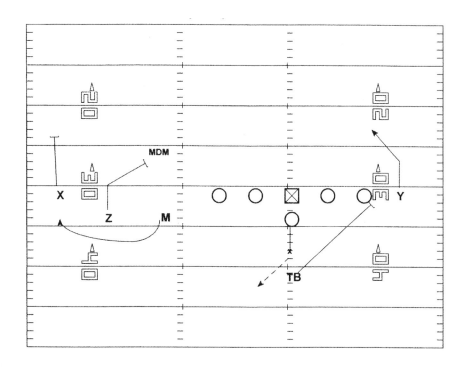

O-Line	Lion call
Y	Run a slant route
Z	Block MDM
X	Drive block the corner
TB	Block the C-gap opposite the line protection call
M	Run a bubble route
QB	Take a 3-step drop; drift to the side of the throw in case of a fumble

Play #3—Trips Left 40 Z Bubble

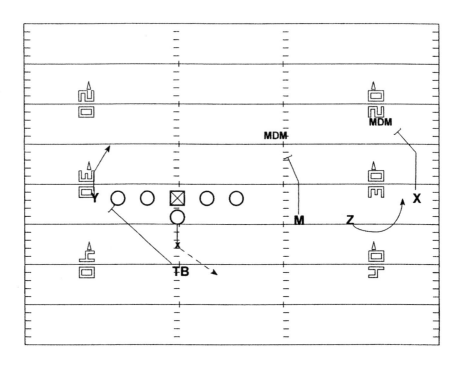

O-Line	Ram call
Y	Run a slant route
Z	Run a bubble route
X	Block MDM
TB	Block the C-gap opposite the line protection call
M	Block MDM
QB	Take a 3-step drop; drift back to the side of the throw to cover in case of a fumble

Play #4—Trey Right 40 M Bubble

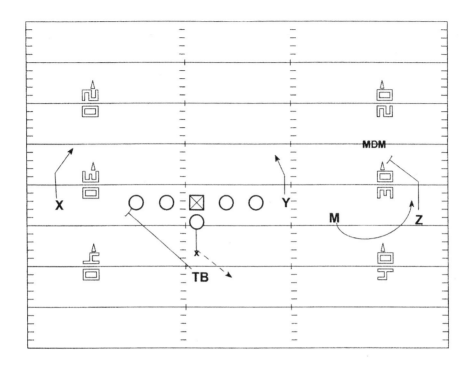

O-Line	Ram call
Y	Run a slant route
Z	Block MDM
X	Run a slant route
TB	Block the C-gap opposite the line protection call
M	Run a bubble route
QB	Take a 3-step drop; drift back to the side of the throw to cover in case of a fumble

Play #5—Doubles Right 40 Bubble

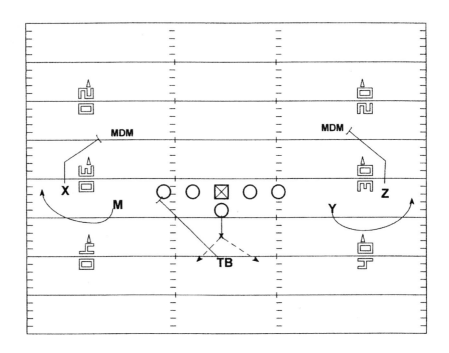

O-Line	Ram call
Y	Run a bubble route
Z	Block MDM
X	Block MDM
TB	Block the C-gap opposite the line protection call
M	Run a bubble route
QB	Choose the best side or match-up; take a 3-step drop; drift to the side of the throw to cover in case of a fumble

2

40 Fast Package—TB

Concept: A bubble route by the tailback from an alignment behind the quarterback, trying to gain a leverage advantage on the defense

Quarterback drop timing: Three steps and fade to ensure that the pass is thrown forward

Key thoughts: Can run to the multiple-receiver side or can run to the side of one of the receivers and run a bubble screen away and read the best possible match-up.

Play #:

6. Queen Left Twins 40 Fast 40 Bubble
7. Trey Right 40 Fast
8. Trips Left 40 Fast
9. Trey Right 40 Fast 44
10. Queen Left Twins 40 Fast

Play #6—Queen Left Twins 40 Fast 40 Bubble

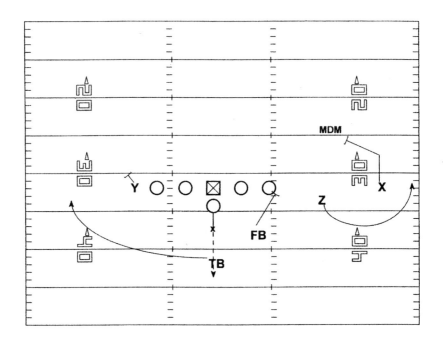

O-Line	Ram call
Y	Block the edge
Z	Run a bubble route
X	Block MDM
TB	Run a bubble route
FB	Block the edge to his side
QB	Take a 3-step drop and fade back to ensure that the pass is thrown forward

Play #7—Trey Right 40 Fast

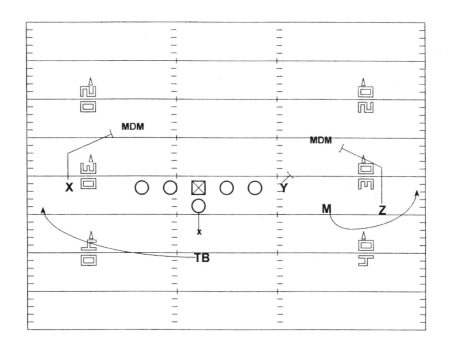

O-Line	Lion call
Y	Block the edge
Z	Block MDM
X	Block MDM
TB	Run a bubble route
M	Run a bubble route
QB	Pick the best side or match-up; take a 3-step drop; fade back to ensure that the pass is thrown forward

Play #8—Trips Left 40 Fast

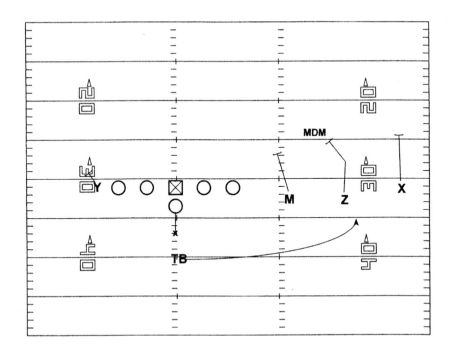

O-Line	Lion call
Y	Block the edge
Z	Block MDM
X	Block the defender head-up
TB	Run a bubble route
M	Block the first defender that shows
QB	Take a 3-step drop; fade back to ensure that the pass is thrown forward

Play #9—Trey Right 40 Fast 44

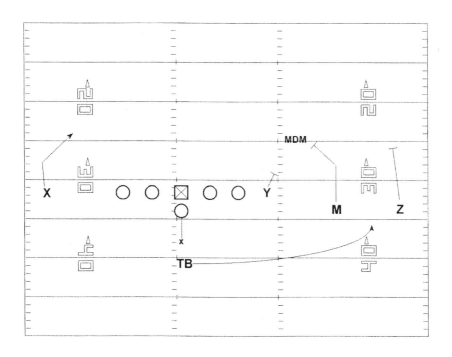

O-Line	Lion call
Y	Block the edge
Z	Block the defender that is head-up
X	Run a slant route
TB	Run a bubble route
M	Block MDM
QB	Choose the best side of match-up; take a 3-step drop

Play #10—Queen Left Twins 40 Fast

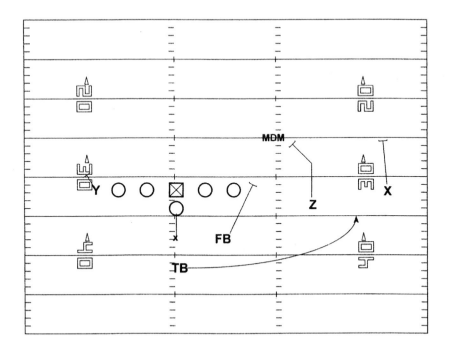

O-Line	Lion call
Y	Block the edge
Z	Block MDM
X	Block the defender that is head-up
TB	Run a bubble route
FB	Block the edge to his side
QB	Take a 3-step drop; fade back to ensure that the pass is thrown forward

3

41 Quick-Out Package

Concept: A quick speed-cut route by the tailback to take advantage of loose flat coverage

Quarterback drop timing: Three steps

Key thoughts: The wide receivers run a three-step speed-cut. The inside receivers run seam routes to hold the curl/flat defenders as long as possible.

Play #:

11. Queen Right 41

12. Queen Right Twins 41

13. Trey Right 41

14. Trips Right 41

15. Doubles Right 41

16. Spread Right 41

17. Duo Right 41

Play #11—Queen Right 41

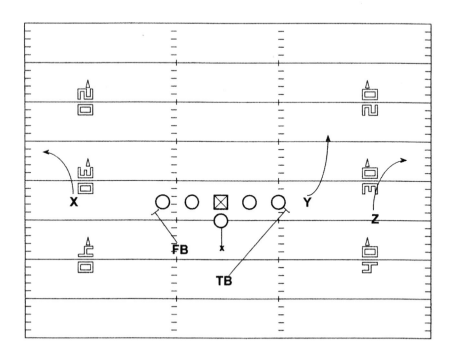

O-Line	Lion call
Y	Run a seam route
Z	Run a speed-cut out
X	Run a speed-cut out
TB	Block the C-gap opposite the line protection call
FB	Block the edge to his side
QB	Pick the best match-up or the softest flat coverage; take a 3-step drop

Play #12—Queen Right Twins 41

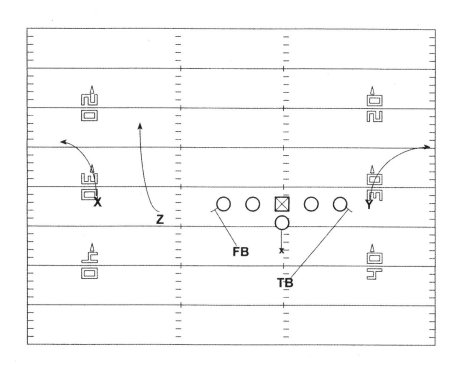

O Line	Lion call
Y	Run a speed-cut out
Z	Run a seam route
X	Run a speed-cut out
TB	Block the C-gap opposite the line protection call
FB	Block the edge
QB	Take a 3-step drop

Play #13—Trey Right 41

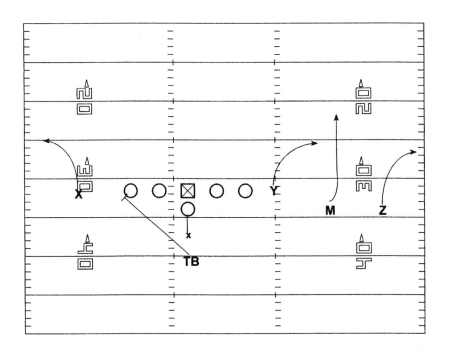

O-Line	Ram call
Y	Run a speed-cut out
Z	Run a speed-cut out
X	Run a speed-cut out
TB	Block the C-gap opposite the line protection call
M	Run a seam route
QB	Take a 3-step drop

Play #14—Trips Right 41

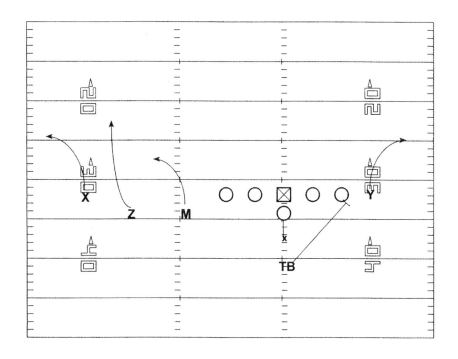

O-Line	Lion call
Y	Run a speed-cut out
Z	Run a seam route
X	Run a speed-cut out
TB	Block the C-gap opposite the line protection call
M	Run a speed-cut out
QB	Take a 3-step drop

Play #15—Doubles Right 41

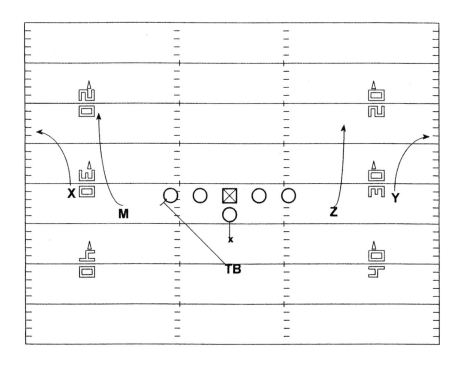

O-Line	Ram call
Y	Run a speed-cut out
Z	Run a seam route
X	Run a speed-cut out
TB	Block the C-gap opposite the line protection call
M	Run a seam route
QB	Take a 3-step drop

Play #16—Spread Right 41

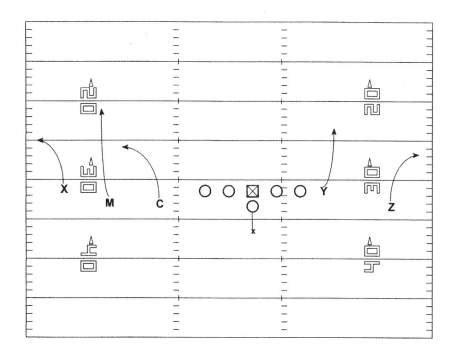

O Line	Lion call
Y	Run a seam route
Z	Run a speed-cut out
X	Run a speed-cut out
C	Run a speed-cut out
M	Run a seam route
QB	Take a 3-step drop

Play #17—Duo Right 41

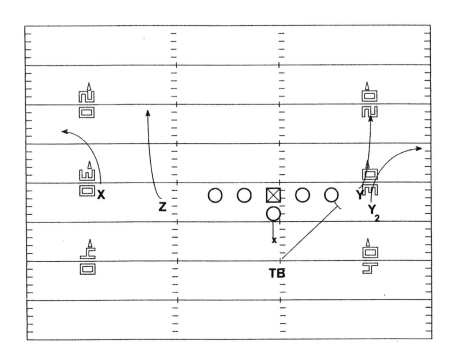

O-Line	Lion call
Y	Run a seam route
Z	Run a seam route
X	Run a speed-cut out
TB	Block the C-gap opposite the line protection call
Y2	Run a speed-cut out
QB	Take a 3-step drop

4

41 Double Quick-Outs

Concept: Execute a "double" tag call in order to alert the two outside most eligible receivers to both sides to run quick speed-cut routes

Quarterback drop timing: Three steps

Key thoughts: The two outside receivers run a three-step speed-cut. The inside most receiver runs a seam. This concept is used to take advantage of soft corner coverage and put pressure on the curl/flat defenders.

Play #:

18. Queen Left Twins 41 Double
19. Deuce Left 41 Double
20. Trey Right 41 Double
21. Doubles Right 41 Double
22. Trips Left 41 Double
23. Spread Right 41 Double

Play #18—Queen Left Twins 41 Double

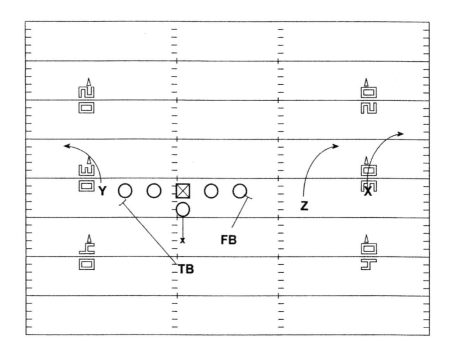

O-Line	Ram call
Y	Run a speed-cut out
Z	Run a speed-cut out
X	Run a speed-cut out
TB	Block the C-gap opposite the line protection call
FB	Block the edge
QB	Take a 3-step drop

Play #19—Deuce Left 41 Double

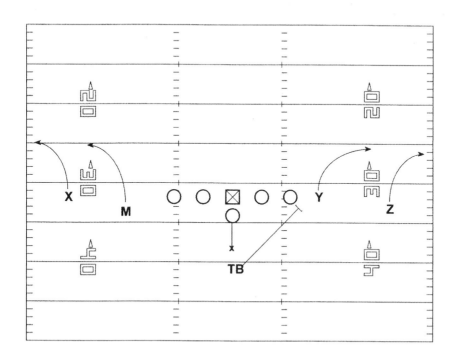

O-Line	Ram call
Y	Run a speed-cut out
Z	Run a speed-cut out
X	Run a speed-cut out
TB	Block the C-gap opposite the line protection call
M	Run a speed-cut out
QB	Take a 3-step drop

Play #20—Trey Right 41 Double

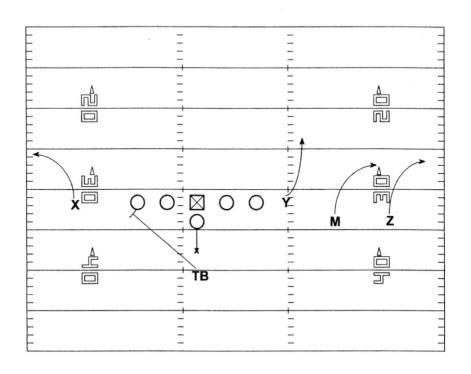

O-Line	Ram call
Y	Run a seam route
Z	Run a speed-cut out
X	Run a speed-cut out
TB	Block the C-gap opposite the line protection call
M	Run a speed-cut out
QB	Take a 3-step drop

Play #21—Doubles Right 41 Double

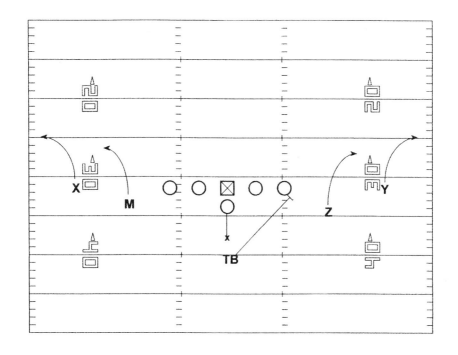

O-Line	Ram call
Y	Run a speed-cut out
Z	Run a speed-cut out
X	Run a speed-cut out
TB	Block the C-gap opposite the line protection call
M	Run a speed-cut out
QB	Take a 3-step drop

Play #22—Trips Left 41 Double

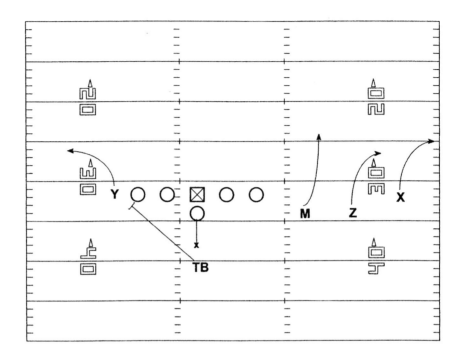

O-Line	Ram call
Y	Run a speed-cut out
Z	Run a speed-cut out
X	Run a speed-cut out
TB	Block the C-gap opposite the line protection call
M	Run a seam route
QB	Take a 3-step drop

Play #23—Spread Right 41 Double

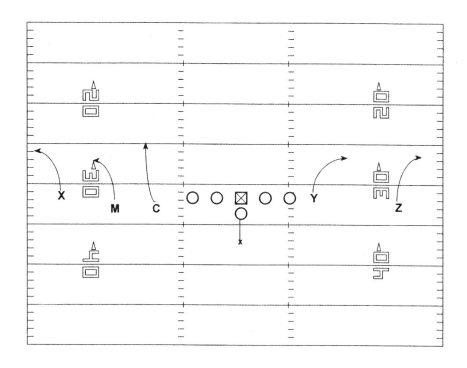

O-Line	Lion call
Y	Run a speed-cut out
Z	Run a speed-cut out
X	Run a speed-cut out
C	Run a seam route
M	Run a speed-cut out
QB	Take a 3-step drop

5

41 Switch Quick-Outs

Concept: Execute a "switch"-tag call in order to alert the eligible receivers to both sides that they are to exchange route responsibilities. The outside most receiver runs a fade and the inside receiver runs the quick speed out. If a third receiver exists to one side of the formation, the route is a seam.

Quarterback drop timing: Three steps

Key thoughts: The quarterback should throw this ball somewhere between a number one (straight line) and a number two (little hump) trajectory if throwing the speed out to the slot receiver. This concept is used to take advantage of soft corner coverage and put pressure on the curl/flat defenders.

Play #:

24. Queen Left Twins 41 Switch
25. Deuce Right 41 Switch
26. Trey Right 41 Switch
27. Doubles Right 41 Switch
28. Trips Right 41 Switch
29. Spread Right 41 Switch
30. Trey Right Spread 41 Switch

Play #24—Queen Right Twins 41 Switch

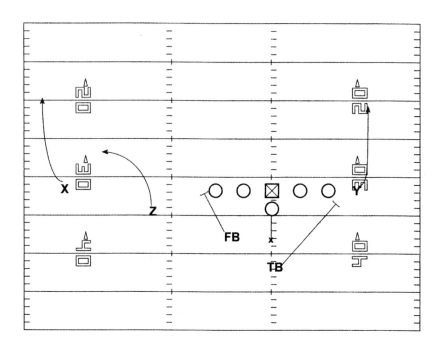

O-Line	Lion call
Y	Run a seam route
Z	Run a speed-cut out
X	Run a fade route
TB	Block the C-gap opposite the line protection call
FB	Block the edge
QB	Take a 3-step drop

Play #25—Deuce Right 41 Switch

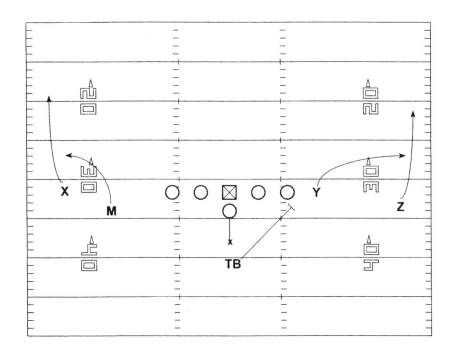

O-Line	Lion call
Y	Run a speed-cut out
Z	Run a fade route
X	Run a fade route
TB	Block the C-gap opposite the line protection call
M	Run a speed-cut out
QB	Take a 3-step drop

Play #26—Trey Right 41 Switch

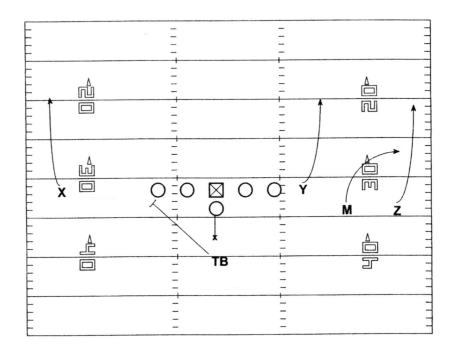

O-Line	Ram call
Y	Run a seam route
Z	Run a fade route
X	Run a fade route
TB	Block the C-gap opposite the line protection call
M	Run a speed-cut out
QB	Take a 3-step drop

Play #27—Doubles Right 41 Switch

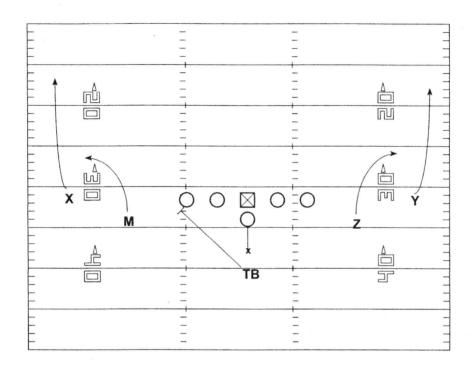

O-Line	Lion call
Y	Run a fade route
Z	Run a speed-cut out
X	Run a fade route
TB	Block the C-gap opposite the line protection call
M	Run a speed-cut out
QB	Take a 3-step drop

Play #28—Trips Right 41 Switch

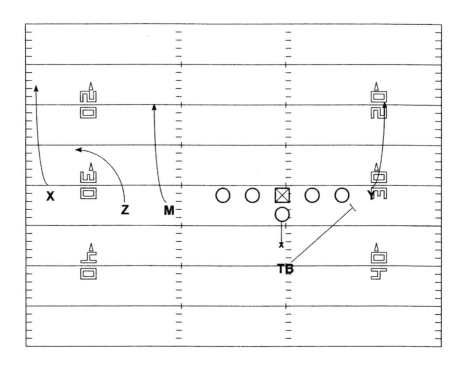

O-Line	Lion call
Y	Run a seam route
Z	Run a speed-cut out
X	Run a fade route
TB	Block the C-gap opposite the line protection call
M	Run a seam route
QB	Take a 3-step drop

Play #29—Spread Right 41 Switch

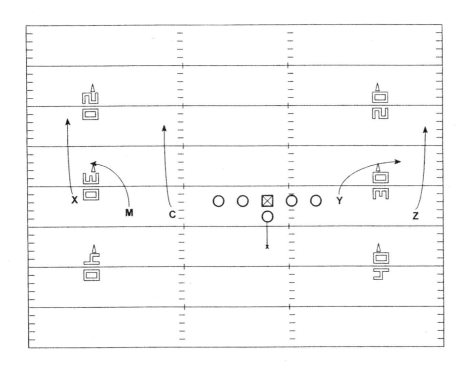

O-Line	Lion call
Y	Run a speed-cut out
Z	Run a fade route
X	Run a fade route
C	Run a seam route
M	Run a speed-cut out
QB	Take a 3-step drop

Play #30—Trey Right Spread 41 Switch

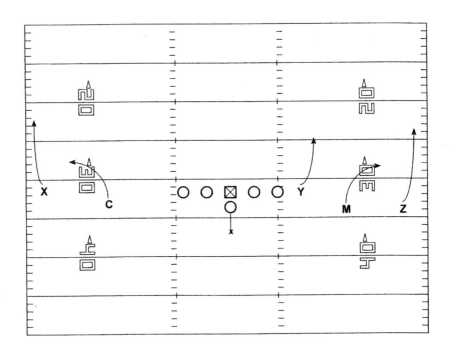

O-Line	Ram call
Y	Run a seam route
Z	Run a fade route
X	Run a fade route
C	Run a speed-cut out
M	Run a speed-cut out
QB	Take a 3-step drop

6

42 Quick-Hitch Package

Concept: A quick-hitch cut to take advantage of loose flat/soft corner coverage

Quarterback drop timing: Three steps

Key thoughts: The wide receivers run a four-step hitch-cut. The inside receivers run seam routes to hold the curl/flat defenders as long as possible.

Play #:

31. Queen Right 42
32. Deuce Right 42
33. Trips Right 42
34. Trey Right 42
35. Doubles Right 42
36. Trey Right Spread 42
37. Spread Right 42

Play #31—Queen Right 42

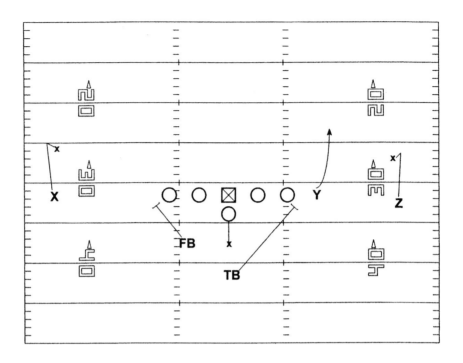

O-Line	Lion call
Y	Run a seam route
Z	Run a quick-hitch cut
X	Run a quick-hitch cut
TB	Block the C-gap opposite the line protection call
FB	Block the edge
QB	Take a 3-step drop

Play #32—Deuce Right 42

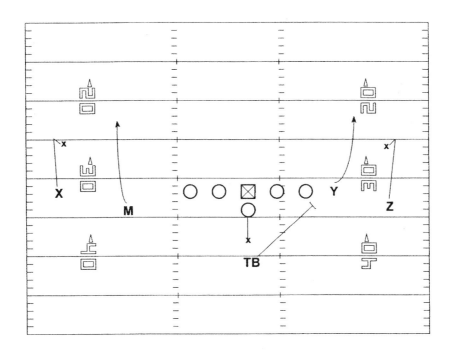

O-Line	Lion call
Y	Run a seam route
Z	Run a quick-hitch cut
X	Run a quick-hitch cut
TB	Block the C-gap opposite the line protection call
M	Run a seam route
QB	Take a 3-step drop

Play #33—Trips Right 42

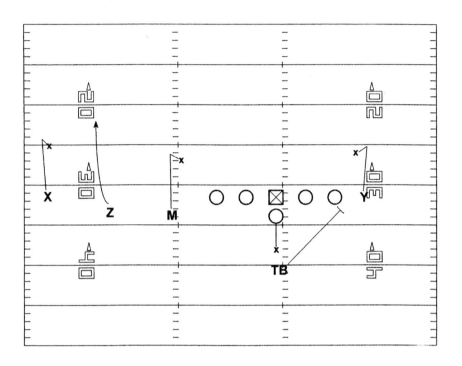

O-Line	Lion call
Y	Run a quick-hitch cut
Z	Run a seam route
Ẋ	Run a quick-hitch cut
TB	Block the C-gap opposite the line protection call
M	Run a quick-hitch cut
QB	Take a 3-step drop

Play #34—Trey Right 42

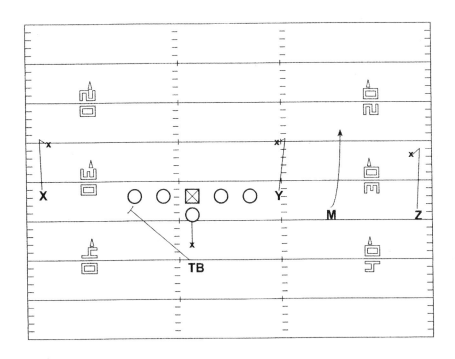

O-Line	Ram call
Y	Run a quick-hitch cut
Z	Run a quick-hitch cut
X	Run a quick-hitch cut
TB	Block the C-gap opposite the line protection call
M	Run a seam route
QB	Take a 3-step drop

Play #35—Doubles Right 42

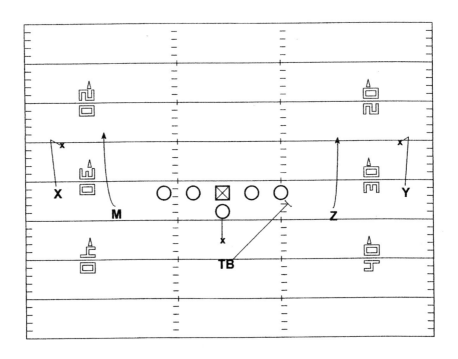

O-Line	Lion call
Y	Run a quick-hitch cut
Z	Run a seam route
X	Run a quick-hitch cut
TB	Block the C-gap opposite the line protection call
M	Run a seam route
QB	Take a 3-step drop

Play #36—Trey Right Spread 42

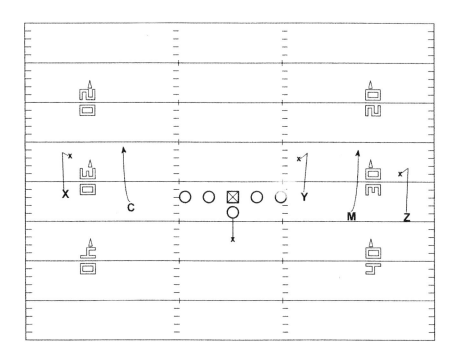

O-Line	Ram call
Y	Run a quick-hitch cut
Z	Run a quick-hitch cut
X	Run a quick-hitch cut
C	Run a seam route
M	Run a seam route
QB	Take a 3-step drop

Play #37—Spread Right 42

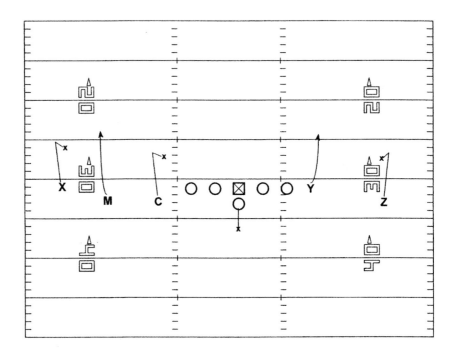

O-Line	Lion call
Y	Run a seam route
Z	Run a quick-hitch cut
X	Run a quick-hitch cut
C	Run a quick-hitch cut
M	Run a seam route
QB	Take a 3-step drop

7

42 Double Quick-Hitches

Concept: The "double" tag will alert the two outside most eligible receivers to both sides to run quick-hitches

Quarterback drop timing: Three steps

Key thoughts: The two outside receivers run a four-step quick-hitch. The inside most receivers run a seam. This concept is used to take advantage of soft corner coverage and put pressure on the curl/flat defenders.

Play #:

38. Queen Right Twins 42 Double

39. Deuce Right 42 Double

40. Trips Right 42 Double

41. Trey Right 42 Double

42. Doubles Right 42 Double

43. Trey Right Spread 42 Double

44. Spread Right 42 Double

Play #38—Queen Right Twins 42 Double

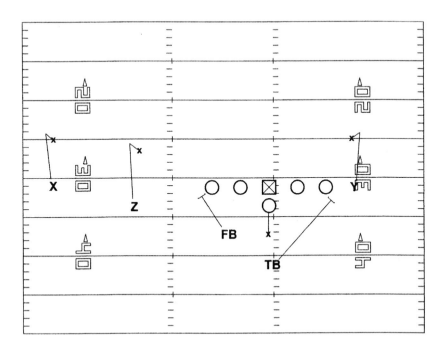

O-Line	Lion call
Y	Run a quick-hitch
Z	Run a quick-hitch
X	Run a quick-hitch
TB	Block the C-gap opposite the line protection call
FB	Block the edge
QB	Take a 3-step drop

Play #39—Deuce Right 42 Double

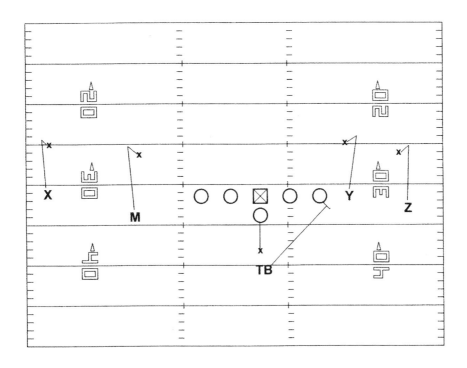

O-Line	Lion call
Y	Run a quick-hitch
Z	Run a quick-hitch
X	Run a quick-hitch
TB	Block the C-gap opposite the line protection call
M	Run a quick-hitch
QB	Take a 3-step drop

Play #40—Trips Right 42 Double

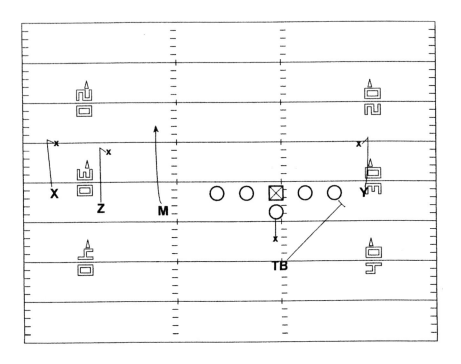

O-Line	Lion call
Y	Run a quick-hitch
Z	Run a quick-hitch
X	Run a quick-hitch
TB	Block the C-gap opposite the line protection call
M	Run a seam route
QB	Take a 3-step drop

Play #41—Trey Right 42 Double

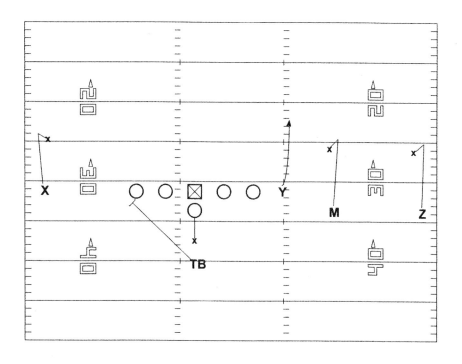

O-Line	Ram call
Y	Run a seam route
Z	Run a quick-hitch
X	Run a quick-hitch
TB	Block the C-gap opposite the line protection call
M	Run a quick-hitch
QB	Take a 3-step drop

Play #42—Doubles Right 42 Double

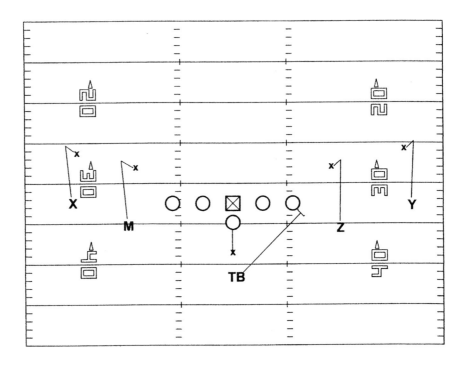

O-Line	Lion call
Y	Run a quick-hitch
Z	Run a quick-hitch
X	Run a quick-hitch
TB	Block the C-gap opposite the line protection call
M	Run a quick-hitch
QB	Take a 3-step drop

Play #43—Trey Right Spread 42 Double

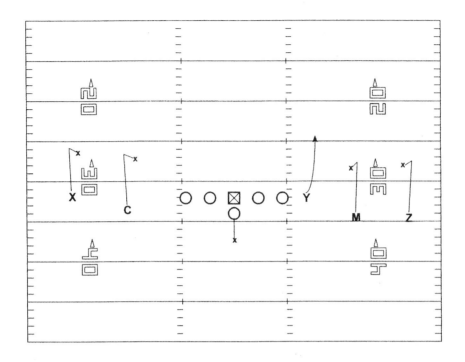

O-Line	Ram call
Y	Run a seam route
Z	Run a quick-hitch
X	Run a quick-hitch
C	Run a quick-hitch
M	Run a quick-hitch
QB	Take a 3-step drop

Play #44—Spread Right 42 Double

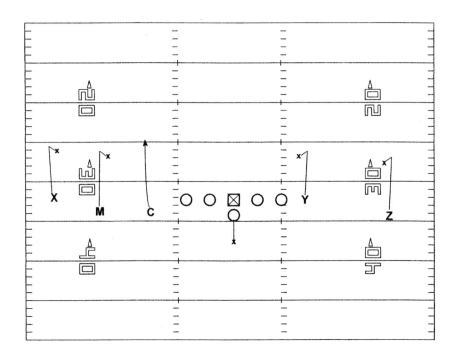

O-Line	Lion call
Y	Run a quick-hitch
Z	Run a quick-hitch
X	Run a quick-hitch
C	Run a seam route
M	Run a quick-hitch
QB	Take a 3-step drop

8

43 Quick-Fade Package

Concept: A quick-fade cut route to take advantage of press man coverage, two, and three-deep zone

Quarterback drop timing: Three steps

Key thoughts: The outside receivers run fade routes on the numbers; the inside receivers run equidistant seam routes to put pressure on the third-level (deep) coverage. The quarterback should throw the ball on a level-two trajectory.

Play #:

45. Queen Right 43

46. Deuce Right 43

47. Trey Right 43

48. Trips Right 43

Play #45—Queen Right 43

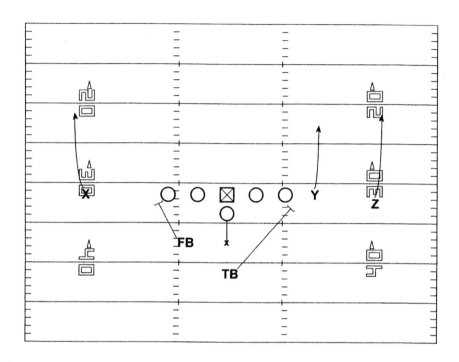

O-Line	Lion call
Y	Run a seam route
Z	Run a fade route
X	Run a fade route
TB	Block the C-gap opposite the line protection call
FB	Block the edge
QB	Take a 3-step drop; throw the ball on a level-two trajectory

Play #46—Deuce Right 43

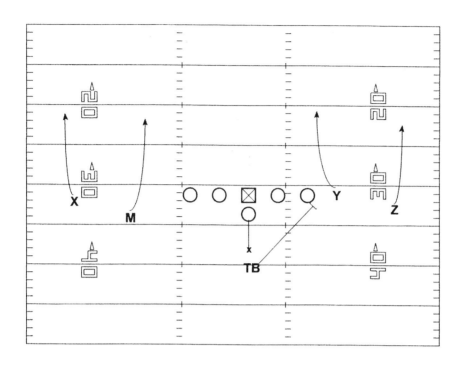

O-Line	Lion call
Y	Run a seam route
Z	Run a fade route
X	Run a fade route
TB	Block the C-gap opposite the line protection call
M	Run a seam route
QB	Take a 3-step drop

Play #47—Trey Right 43

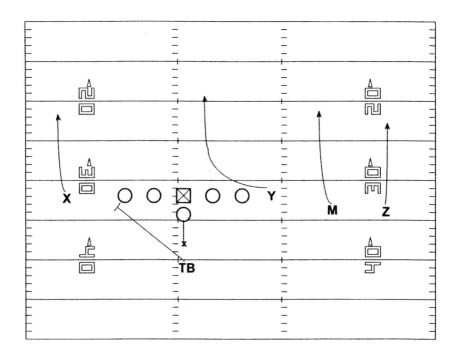

O-Line	Ram call
Y	Run a seam route, keeping proper spacing to stretch the safeties
Z	Run a fade route
X	Run a fade route
TB	Block the C-gap opposite the line protection call
M	Run a seam route
QB	Take a 3-step drop

Play #48—Trips Right 43

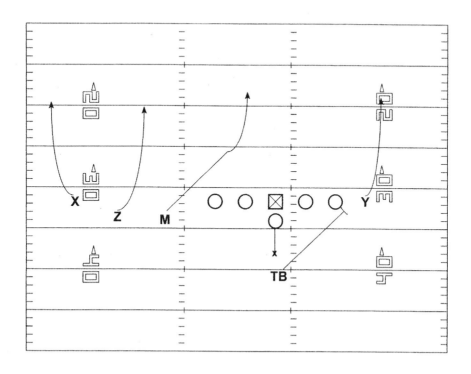

O-Line	Lion call
Y	Run a fade route
Z	Run a seam route
X	Run a fade route
TB	Block the C-gap opposite the line protection call
M	Run a seam route, keeping proper spacing to create stretch on the safeties
QB	Take a 3-step drop

9

44 Quick-Slant Package

Concept: A quick-slant cut route to take advantage of press man coverage and the curl/flat defender

Quarterback drop timing: Three steps

Key thoughts: The outside receivers run quick-slant routes on their third step; the inside receivers run arrow routes at approximately three yards. The quarterback reads the curl/flat coverage.

Play #:

49. Queen Right 44
50. Deuce Right 44
51. Spread Right 44
52. Trey Right 44
53. Doubles Right 44
54. Trips Right 44
55. Queen Right Twins 44

Play #49—Queen Right 44

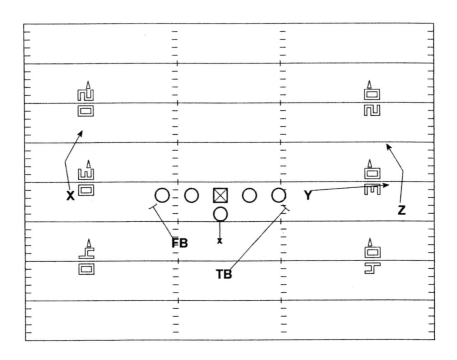

O-Line	Lion call
Y	Run an arrow route
Z	Run a quick-slant route
X	Run a quick-slant route
TB	Block the C-gap opposite the line protection call
FB	Block the edge
QB	Take a 3-step drop

Play #50—Deuce Right 44

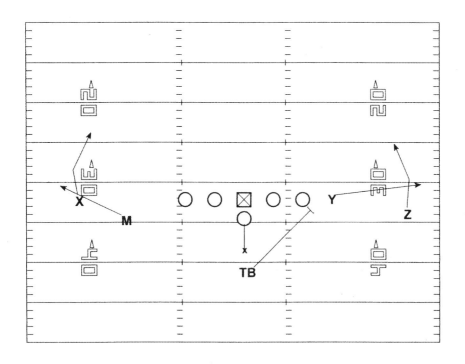

O-Line	Lion call
Y	Run an arrow route
Z	Run a quick-slant route
X	Run a quick-slant route
TB	Block the C-gap opposite the line protection call
M	Run an arrow route
QB	Take a 3-step drop

Play #51—Spread Right 44

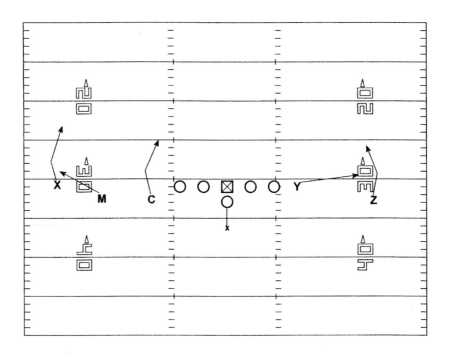

O-Line	Lion call
Y	Run an arrow route
Z	Run a quick-slant route
X	Run a quick-slant route
C	Run a quick-slant route
M	Run an arrow route
QB	Take a 3-step drop

Play #52—Trey Right 44

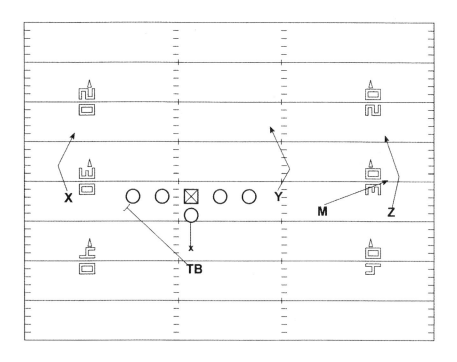

O-Line	Ram call
Y	Run a quick-slant route
Z	Run a quick-slant route
X	Run a quick-slant route
TB	Block the C-gap opposite the line protection call
M	Run an arrow route
QB	Take a 3-step drop

Play #53—Doubles Right 44

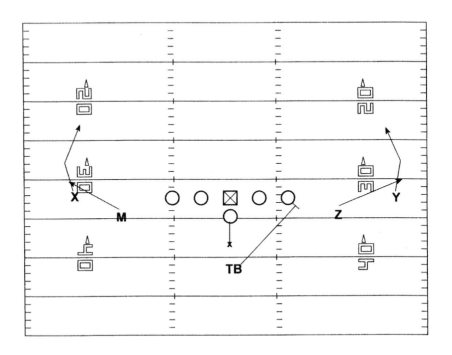

O-Line	Lion call
Y	Run a quick-slant route
Z	Run an arrow route
X	Run a quick-slant route
TB	Block the C-gap opposite the line protection call
M	Run an arrow route
QB	Take a 3-step drop

Play #54—Trips Right 44

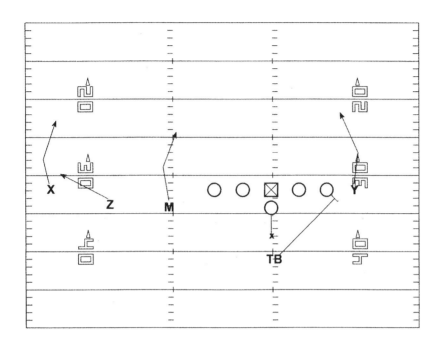

O-Line	Lion call
Y	Run a quick-slant route
Z	Run an arrow route
X	Run a quick-slant route
TB	Block the C-gap opposite the line protection call
M	Run a quick-slant route
QB	Take a 3-step drop

Play #55—Queen Right Twins 44

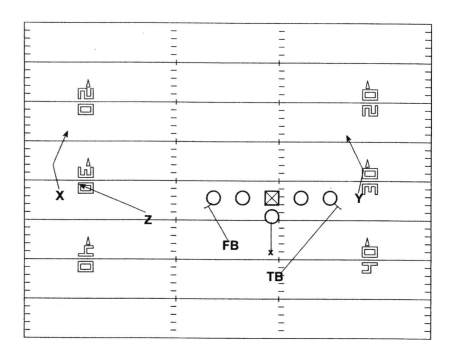

O-Line	Lion call
Y	Run a quick-slant route
Z	Run an arrow route
X	Run a quick-slant route
TB	Block the C-gap opposite the line protection call
FB	Block the edge
QB	Take a 3-step drop

10

44 Double Quick-Slants

Concept: Double quick-slant cuts to take advantage of the curl/flat defender. Designed to be good against any coverage.

Quarterback drop timing: Three steps

Key thoughts: The two outside most receivers run quick-slants; the inside most receivers run arrow routes at approximately three yards. The inside receiver is trying to clear the flat defender, while the outside receiver must widen his stem to clear the curl/flat area. Proper spacing between the receivers is important.

Play #:

56. Queen Right Twins 44 Double
57. Deuce Right 44 Double
58. Doubles Right 44 Double
59. Trey Right 44 Double
60. Trips Right 44 Double
61. Trey Right Spread 44 Double
62. Spread Right 44 Double

Play #56—Queen Right Twins 44 Double

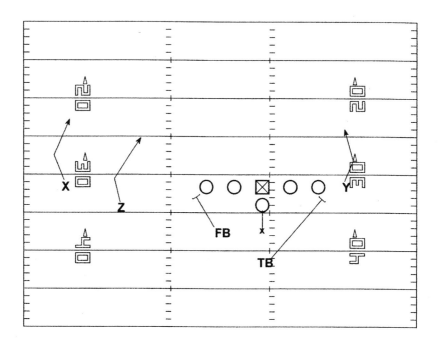

O-Line	Lion call
Y	Run a quick-slant route
Z	Run a quick-slant route
X	Run a quick-slant route
TB	Block the C-gap opposite the line protection call
FB	Block the edge
QB	Take a 3-step drop

Play #57—Deuce Right 44 Double

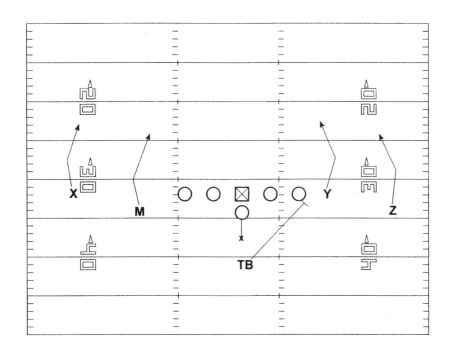

O-Line	Lion call
Y	Run a quick-slant route
Z	Run a quick-slant route
X	Run a quick-slant route
TB	Block the C-gap opposite the line protection call
M	Run a quick-slant route
QB	Take a 3-step drop

Play #58—Doubles Right 44 Double

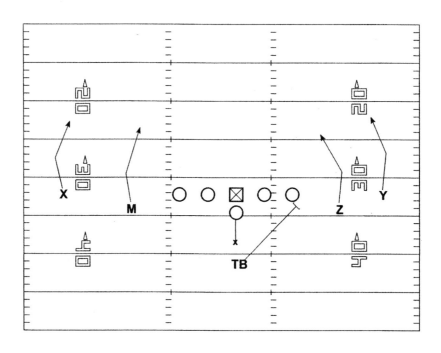

O-Line	Lion call
Y	Run a quick-slant route
Z	Run a quick-slant route
X	Run a quick-slant route
TB	Block the C-gap opposite the line protection call
M	Run a quick-slant route
QB	Take a 3-step drop

Play #59—Trey Right 44 Double

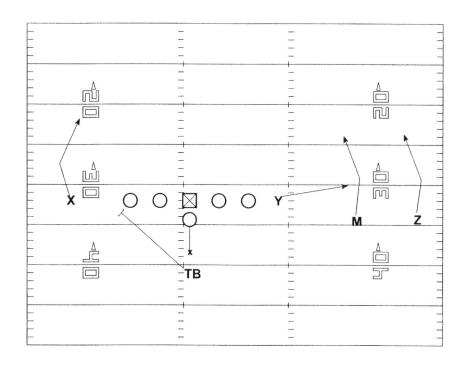

O-Line	Ram call
Y	Run an arrow route
Z	Run a quick-slant route
X	Run a quick-slant route
TB	Block the C-gap opposite the line protection call
M	Run a quick-slant route
QB	Take a 3-step drop

Play #60—Doubles Right 44 Double

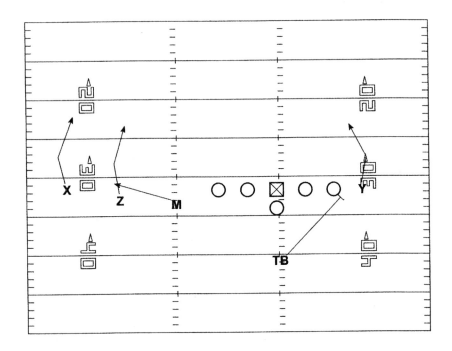

O-Line	Lion call
Y	Run a quick-slant route
Z	Run a quick-slant route
X	Run a quick-slant route
TB	Block the C-gap opposite the line protection call
M	Run an arrow route
QB	Take a 3-step drop

Play #61—Trips Right Spread 44 Double

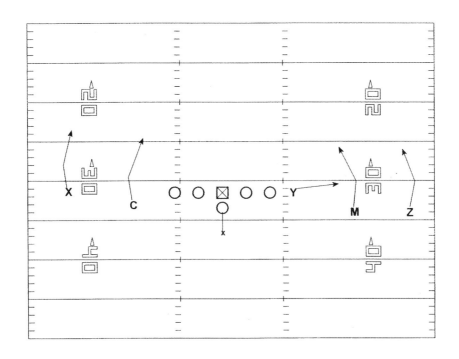

O Line	Ram call
Y	Run an arrow route
Z	Run a quick-slant route
X	Run a quick-slant route
C	Run a quick-slant route
M	Run a quick-slant route
QB	Take a 3-step drop

Play #62—Spread Right 44 Double

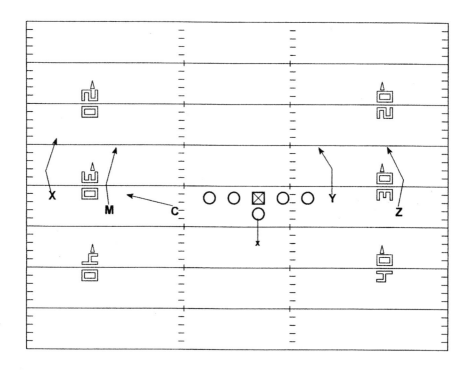

O-Line	Lion call
Y	Run a quick-slant route
Z	Run a quick-slant route
X	Run a quick-slant route
C	Run an arrow route
M	Run a quick-slant route
QB	Take a 3-step drop

11

45 Fade-Stop Package

Concept: A fade-stop route to use on the goal line. Designed to be good against any tight coverage.

Quarterback drop timing: Three steps

Key thoughts: The outside receivers run the fade stop. The inside receivers run a seam. The fade-stop stem should appear as 43 (Quick Fade). At a predetermined point (eight yards), the receiver should stop and angle to the sidelines.

Play #:

63. Queen Right 45

64. Deuce Right 45

65. Trips Right 45

66. Trey Right 45

67. Doubles Right 45

Play #63—Queen Right 45

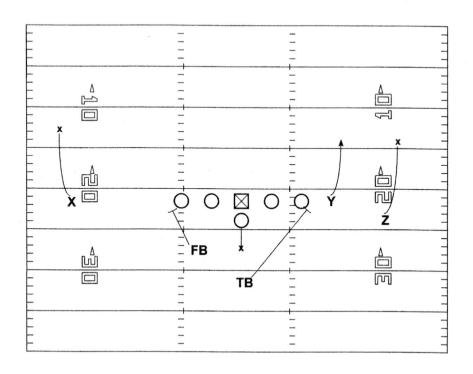

O-Line	Lion call
Y	Run a seam route
Z	Run a fade-stop route
X	Run a fade-stop route
TB	Block the C-gap opposite the line protection call
FB	Block the edge
QB	Take a 3-step drop; throw on a level-one trajectory, aiming for the receiver's backside ear hole

Play #64—Deuce Right 45

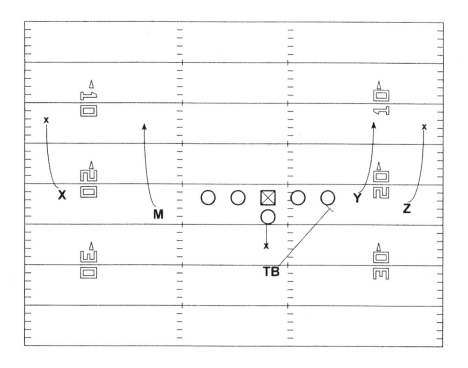

O-Line	Lion call
Y	Run a seam route
Z	Run a fade-stop route
X	Run a fade-stop route
TB	Block the C-gap opposite the line protection call
M	Run a seam route
QB	Take a 3-step drop; throw on a level-one trajectory, aiming for the receiver's backside ear hole

Play #65—Trips Right 45

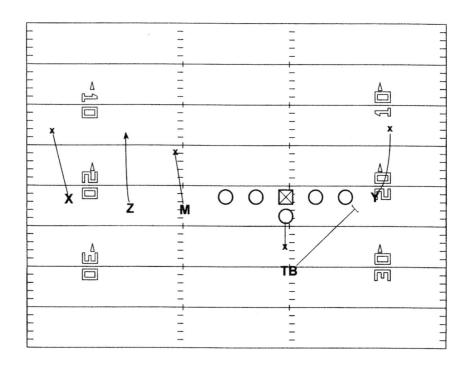

O-Line	Lion call
Y	Run a fade-stop route
Z	Run a seam route
X	Run a fade-stop route
TB	Block the C-gap opposite the line protection call
M	Run a fade-stop route
QB	Take a 3-step drop; throw on a level-one trajectory, aiming for the receiver's backside ear hole

Play #66—Trey Right 45

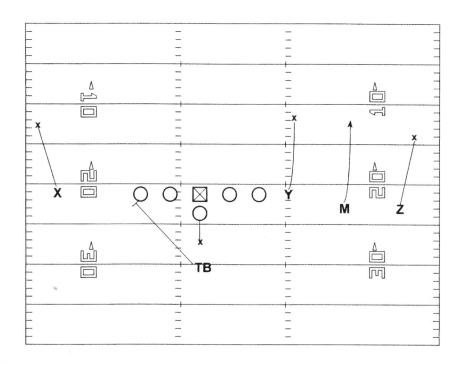

O-Line	Ram call
Y	Run a fade-stop route
Z	Run a fade-stop route
X	Run a fade-stop route
TB	Block the C-gap opposite the line protection call
FB	Run a seam route
QB	Take a 3-step drop; throw on a level-one trajectory, aiming for the receiver's backside ear hole

Play #67—Doubles Right 45

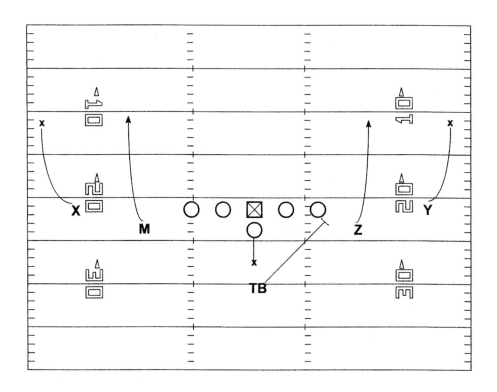

O-Line	Lion call
Y	Run a fade-stop route
Z	Run a seam route
X	Run a fade-stop route
TB	Block the C-gap opposite the line protection call
M	Run a seam route
QB	Take a 3-step drop; throw on a level-one trajectory, aiming for the receiver's backside ear hole

12

45 Double Fade-Stop

Concept: Fade-stop routes to use on the goal line. Designed to be good against any tight coverage.

Quarterback drop timing: Three steps

Key thoughts: The outside most receivers run fade stops. The inside receivers run a seam. The fade-stop stem should appear as 43 (Quick Fade). At a predetermined point (eight yards), the receiver should stop and angle to the sidelines. Proper spacing is a must. The quarterback should read the best match-up.

Play #:

68. Queen Left Twins 45 Double
69. Deuce Right 45 Double
70. Trey Right 45 Double
71. Spread Right 45 Double
72. Trey Right Spread 45 Double

Play #68—Queen Left Twins 45 Double

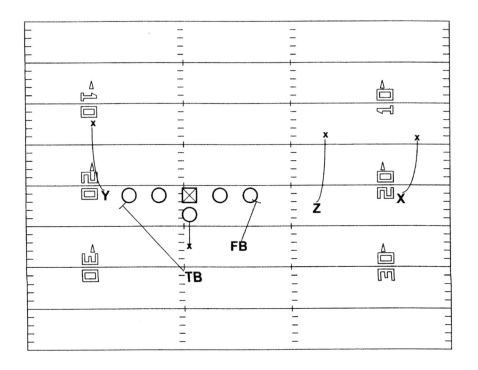

O-Line	Ram call
Y	Run a fade-stop route
Z	Run a fade-stop route
X	Run a fade-stop route
TB	Block the C-gap opposite the line protection call
FB	Block the edge
QB	Take a 3-step drop; throw on a level-one trajectory, aiming for the receiver's backside ear hole

Play #69—Deuce Right 45 Double

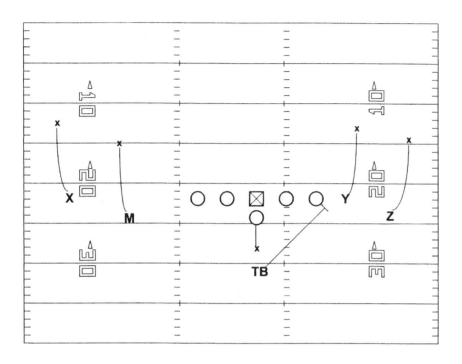

O-Line	Lion call
Y	Run a fade-stop route
Z	Run a fade-stop route
X	Run a fade-stop route
TB	Block the C-gap opposite the line protection call
M	Run a fade-stop route
QB	Take a 3-step drop; throw on a level-one trajectory, aiming for the receiver's backside ear hole

Play #70—Trey Right 45 Double

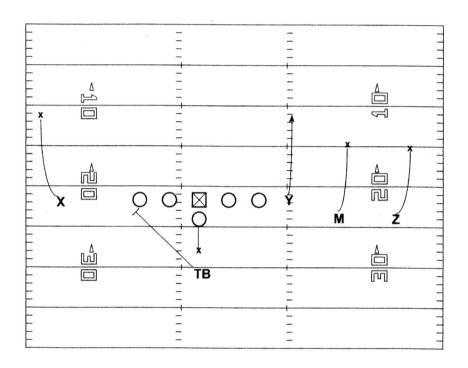

O-Line	Ram call
Y	Run a seam route
Z	Run a fade-stop route
X	Run a fade-stop route
TB	Block the C-gap opposite the line protection call
M	Run a fade-stop route
QB	Take a 3-step drop; throw on a level-one trajectory, aiming for the receiver's backside ear hole

Play #71—Spread Right 45 Double

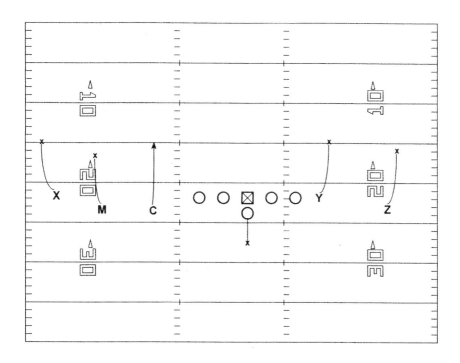

O-Line	Lion call
Y	Run a fade-stop route
Z	Run a fade-stop route
X	Run a fade-stop route
C	Run a seam route
M	Run a fade-stop route
QB	Take a 3-step drop; throw on a level-one trajectory, aiming for the receiver's backside ear hole

Play #72—Trey Right Spread 45 Double

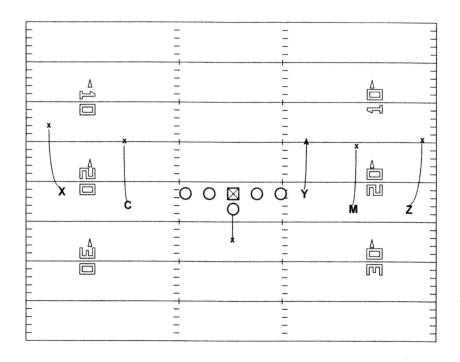

O-Line	Ram call
Y	Run a seam route
Z	Run a fade-stop route
X	Run a fade-stop route
C	Run a fade-stop route
M	Run a fade-stop route
QB	Take a 3-step drop; throw on a level-one trajectory, aiming for the receiver's backside ear hole

13

46 Slant-Vertical Package

Concept: The outside most receivers run the slant-vertical, while the inside receivers run an arrow. Designed to be good versus coverages with no deep-safety help and teams that play the slant aggressively.

Quarterback drop timing. Three steps

Key thoughts: The receivers must avoid a collision with the defensive back on the vertical portion of the stem.

Play #:

73. Queen Right 46
74. Queen Right Twins 46
75. Deuce Right 46
76. Doubles Right 46
77. Trey Right 46
78. Trips Right 46
79. Trey Right Spread 46
80. Spread Right 46

Play #73—Queen Right 46

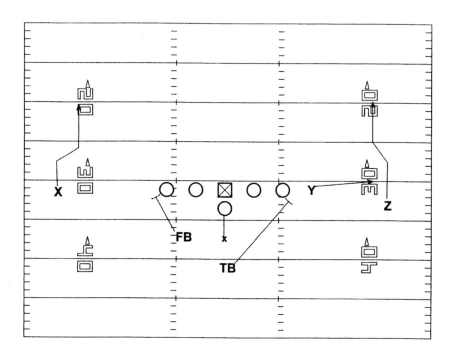

O-Line	Lion call
Y	Run an arrow route
Z	Run a slant-vertical route
X	Run a slant-vertical route
TB	Block the C-gap opposite the line protection call
FB	Block the edge
QB	Take a 3-step drop

Play #74—Queen Right Twins 46

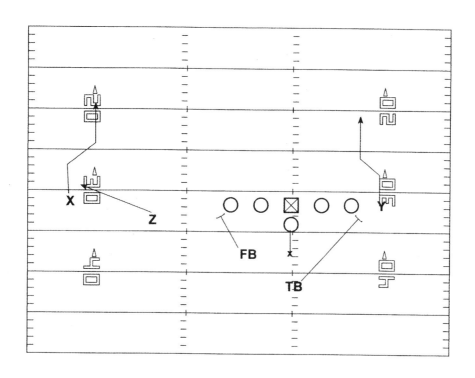

O-line	Lion call
Y	Run a slant-vertical route
Z	Run an arrow route
X	Run a slant-vertical route
TB	Block the C-gap opposite the line protection call
FB	Block the edge
QB	Take a 3-step drop

Play #75—Deuce Right 46

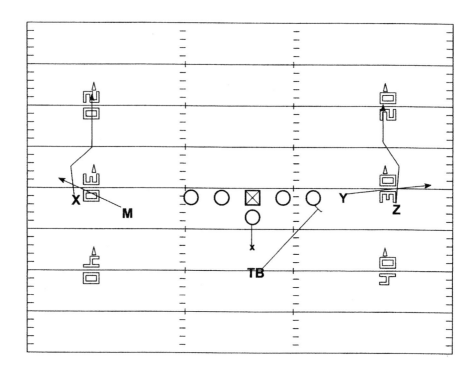

O-Line	Lion call
Y	Run an arrow route
Z	Run a slant-vertical route
X	Run a slant-vertical route
TB	Block the C-gap opposite the line protection call
M	Run a slant-vertical route
QB	Take a 3-step drop

Play #76—Doubles Right 46

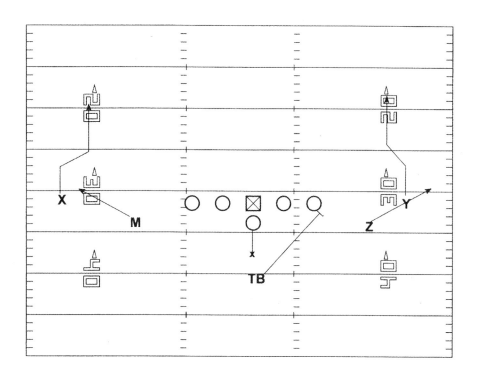

O-Line	Lion call
Y	Run a slant-vertical route
Z	Run an arrow route
X	Run a slant-vertical route
TB	Block the C-gap opposite the line protection call
M	Run an arrow route
QB	Take a 3-step drop

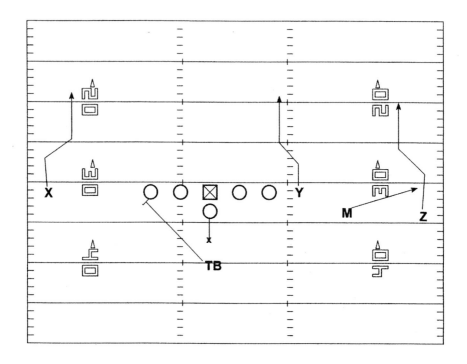

O-Line	Ram call
Y	Run a slant-vertical route
Z	Run a slant-vertical route
X	Run a slant-vertical route
TB	Block the C-gap opposite the line protection call
M	Run a slant-vertical route
QB	Take a 3-step drop

Play #78—Trips Right 46

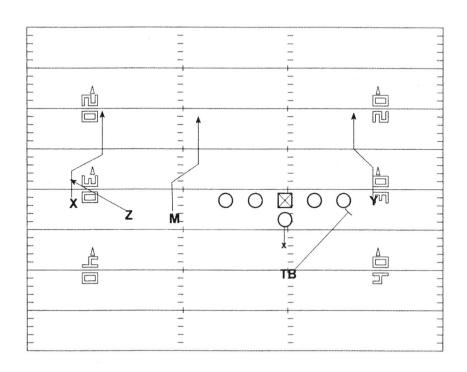

O-Line	Lion call
Y	Run a slant-vertical route
Z	Run an arrow route
X	Run a slant-vertical route
TB	Block the C-gap opposite the line protection call
M	Run a slant-vertical route
QB	Take a 3-step drop

Play #79—Trey Right Spread 46

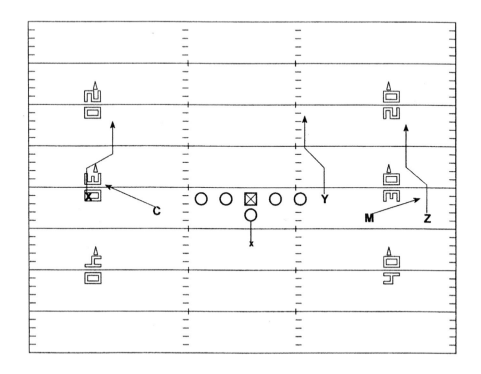

O-Line	Ram call
Y	Run a slant-vertical route
Z	Run a slant-vertical route
X	Run a slant-vertical route
C	Run an arrow route
M	Run an arrow route
QB	Take a 3-step drop

Play #80—Spread Right 46

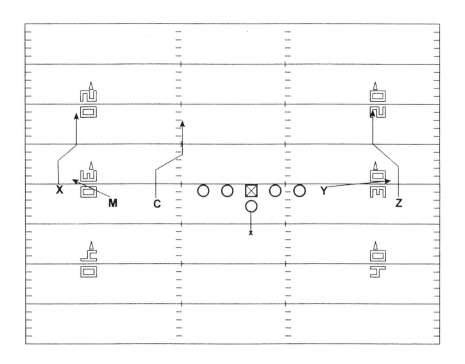

O-Line	Lion call
Y	Run an arrow route
Z	Run a slant-vertical route
X	Run a slant-vertical route
C	Run a slant-vertical route
M	Run an arrow route
QB	Take a 3-step drop

14

46 Double Slant-Vertical

Concept: The two outside most receivers run the slant-vertical, while the inside receivers run an arrow. Designed to be good versus coverages with no deep-safety help and teams that play the slant aggressively.

Quarterback drop timing: Three steps

Key thoughts: The receivers must avoid a collision with the defensive back on the vertical portion of the stem.

Play #:

81. Queen Right Twins 46 Double
82. Trey Right 46 Double
83. Trips Right 46 Double

Play #81—Queen Right Twins 46 Double

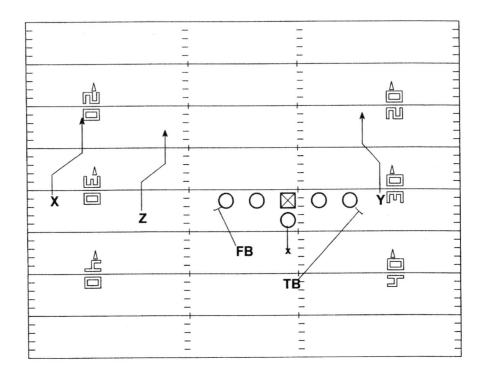

O-Line	Lion call
Y	Run a slant-vertical route
Z	Run a slant-vertical route
X	Run a slant-vertical route
TB	Block the C-gap opposite the line protection call
FB	Block the edge
QB	Take a 3-step drop

Play #82—Trey Right 46 Double

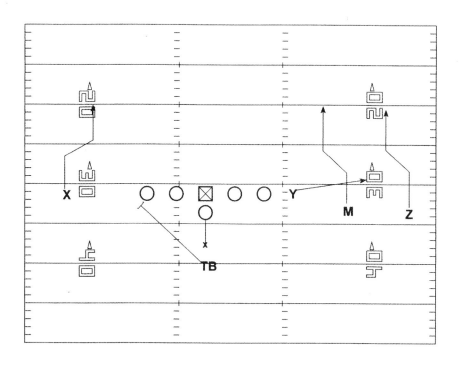

O-Line	Ram call
Y	Run an arrow route
Z	Run a slant-vertical route
X	Run a slant-vertical route
TB	Block the C-gap opposite the line protection call
M	Run a slant-vertical route
QB	Take a 3-step drop

Play #83—Trips Right 46 Double

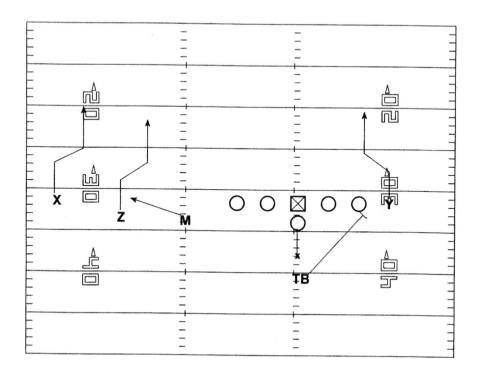

O-Line	Lion call
Y	Run a slant-vertical route
Z	Run a slant-vertical route
X	Run a slant-vertical route
TB	Block the C-gap opposite the line protection call
M	Run an arrow route
QB	Take a 3-step drop

15

47 Quick-Whip Package

Concept: The outside receivers run the whip route, while the inside receivers run a seam. Designed to be good versus three-deep, man, or quarter coverages.

Quarterback drop timing: Three steps

Key thoughts: The receiver's route must look like a slant and sharply break to the flat.

Play #:

84. Queen Right 47
85. Deuce Right 47
86. Trey Right 47
87. Trips Right 47
88. Doubles Right 47
89. Trey Right Spread 47
90. Spread Right 47

Play #84—Queen Right 47

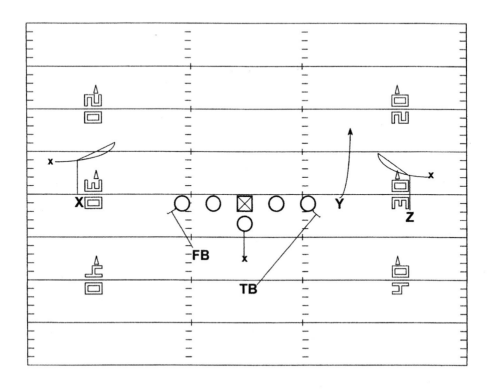

O-Line	Lion call
Y	Run a seam route
Z	Run a whip route
X	Run a whip route
TB	Block the C-gap opposite the line protection call
FB	Block the edge
QB	Take a 3-step drop

Play #85—Deuce Right 47

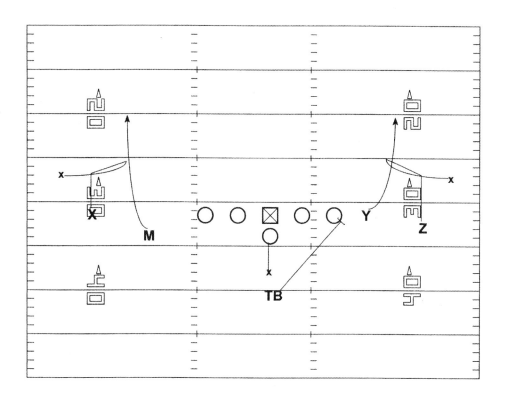

O-Line	Lion call
Y	Run a seam route
Z	Run a whip route
X	Run a whip route
TB	Block the C-gap opposite the line protection call
M	Run a seam route
QB	Take a 3-step drop

Play #86—Trey Right 47

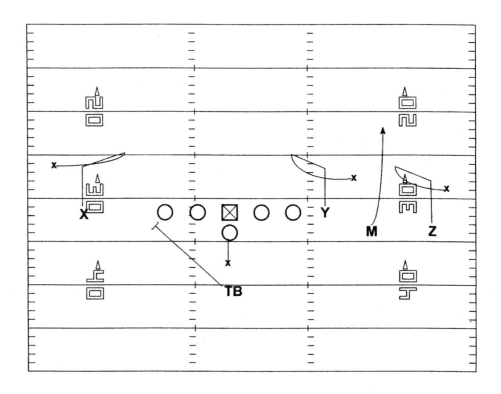

O-Line	Ram call
Y	Run a whip route
Z	Run a whip route
X	Run a whip route
TB	Block the C-gap opposite the line protection call
M	Run a seam route
QB	Take a 3-step drop

Play #87—Trips Right 47

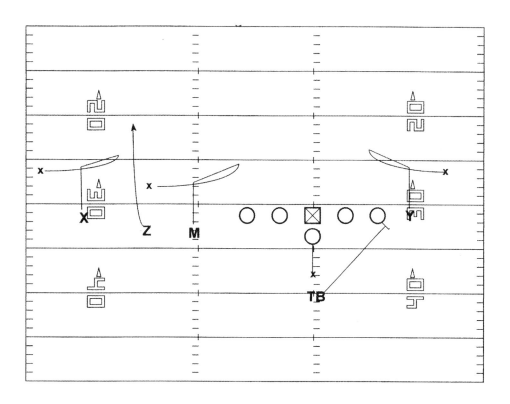

O-Line	Lion call
Y	Run a whip route
Z	Run a seam route
X	Run a whip route
TB	Block the C-gap opposite the line protection call
M	Run a whip route
QB	Take a 3-step drop

Play #88—Doubles Right 47

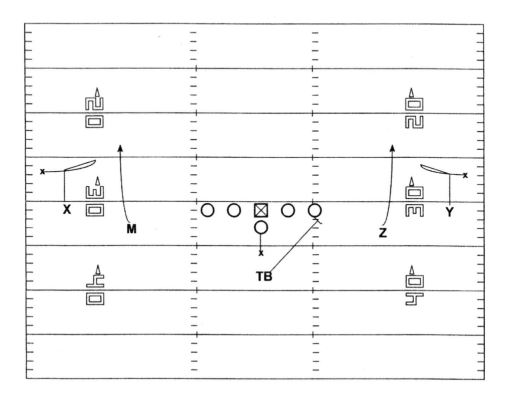

O-Line	Lion call
Y	Run a whip route
Z	Run a seam route
X	Run a whip route
TB	Block the C-gap opposite the line protection call
M	Run a seam route
QB	Take a 3-step drop

Play #89—Trey Right Spread 47

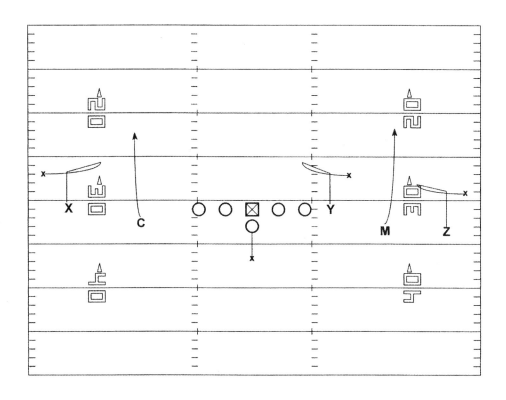

O-Line	Ram call
Y	Run a whip route
Z	Run a whip route
X	Run a whip route
C	Run a seam route
M	Run a seam route
QB	Take a 3-step drop

Play #90—Spread Right 47

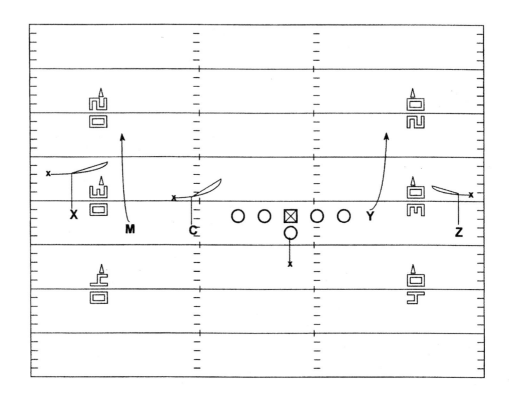

O-Line	Lion call
Y	Run a seam route
Z	Run a whip route
X	Run a whip route
C	Run a whip route
M	Run a seam route
QB	Take a 3-step drop

16

48 Quick-Under Package

Concept: The outside receivers run the under route, while the inside receivers run a corner. Designed to be good versus any zone or tight man coverages.

Quarterback drop timing: Three steps

Key thoughts: The receiver's route must look like a speed-out and convert to an under.

Play #:
91. Deuce Right 48
92. Queen Right Twins 48
93. Trips Right 48
94. Trey Right 48
95. Doubles Right 48

Play #91—Deuce Right 48

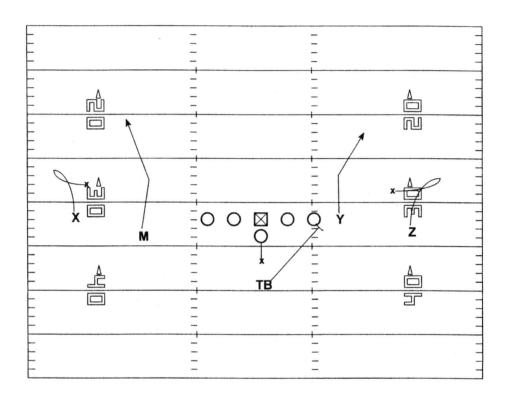

O-Line	Lion call
Y	Run a quick-corner route
Z	Run a quick-under route
X	Run a quick-under route
TB	Block the C-gap opposite the line protection call
M	Run a quick-corner route
QB	Take a 3-step drop

Play #92—Queen Right Twins 48

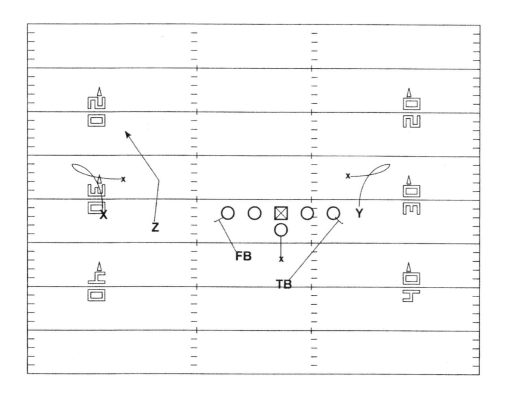

O-Line	Lion call
Y	Run a quick-under route
Z	Run a quick-corner route
X	Run a quick-under route
TB	Block the C-gap opposite the line protection call
FB	Block the edge
QB	Take a 3-step drop

Play #93—Trips Right 48

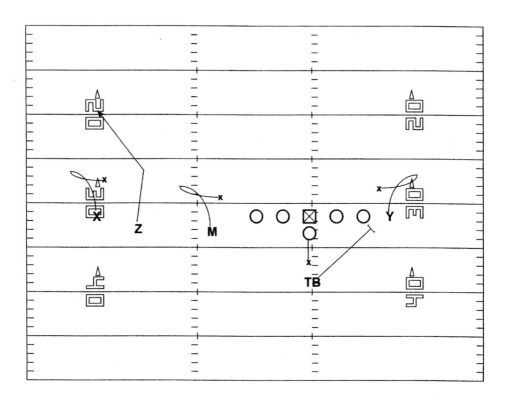

O-Line	Lion call
Y	Run a quick-under route
Z	Run a quick-corner route
X	Run a quick-under route
TB	Block the C-gap opposite the line protection call
M	Run a quick-under route
QB	Take a 3-step drop

Play #94—Trey Right 48

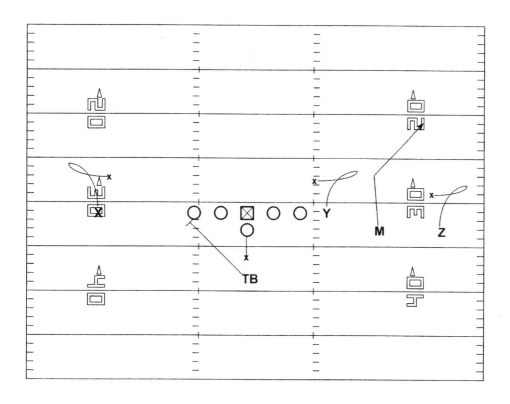

O-Line	Ram call
Y	Run a quick-under route
Z	Run a quick-under route
X	Run a quick-under route
TB	Block the C-gap opposite the line protection call
M	Run a quick-corner route
QB	Take a 3-step drop

Play #95—Doubles Right 48

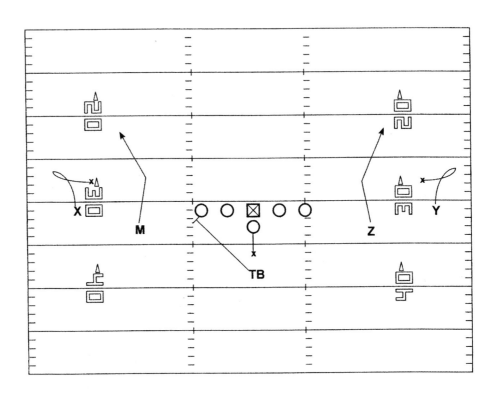

O-Line	Ram call
Y	Run a quick-under route
Z	Run a quick-corner route
X	Run a quick-under route
TB	Block the C-gap opposite the line protection call
M	Run a quick-corner route
QB	Take a 3-step drop

17

49 Quick-Smash Package

Concept: The outside receivers run the smash route, while the inside receivers run a corner. Designed to be good versus any coverage.

Quarterback drop timing: Three steps

Key thoughts: The quarterback will read low-to-high in three-step rhythm.

Play #:

96. Deuce Right 49

97. Trey Right 49

98. Trips Right 49

99. Doubles Right 49

100. Spread Right 49

101. Trey Right Spread 49

Play #96—Deuce Right 49

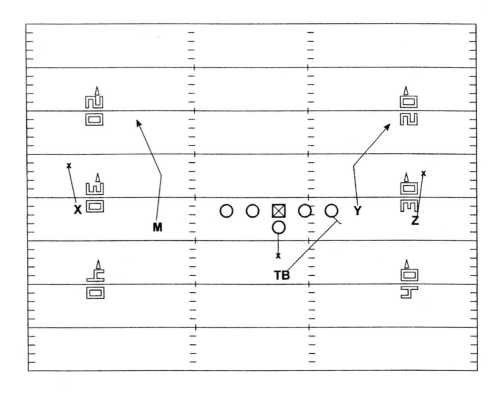

O-Line	Lion call
Y	Run a quick-corner route
Z	Run a smash route
X	Run a smash route
TB	Block the C-gap opposite the line protection call
M	Run a quick-corner route
QB	Take a 3-step drop

Play #97—Trey Right 49

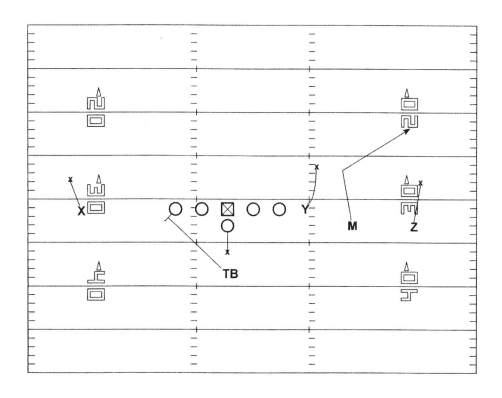

O-Line	Ram call
Y	Run a smash route
Z	Run a smash route
X	Run a smash route
TB	Block the C-gap opposite the line protection call
M	Run a quick-corner route
QB	Take a 3-step drop

Play #98—Trips Right 49

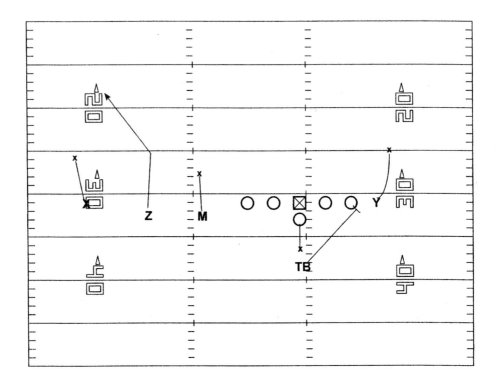

O-Line	Lion call
Y	Run a smash route
Z	Run a quick-corner route
X	Run a smash route
TB	Block the C-gap opposite the line protection call
M	Run a smash route
QB	Take a 3-step drop

Play #99—Doubles Right 49

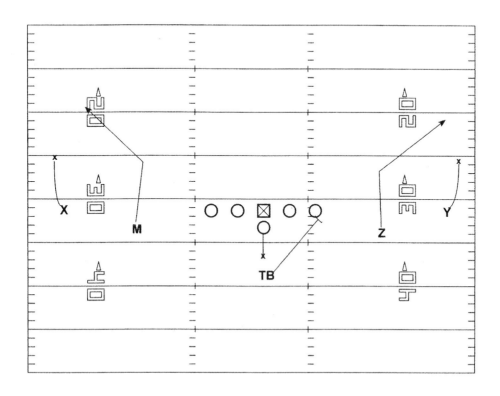

O Line	Lion call
Y	Run a smash route
Z	Run a quick-corner route
X	Run a smash route
TB	Block the C-gap opposite the line protection call
M	Run a quick-corner route
QB	Take a 3-step drop

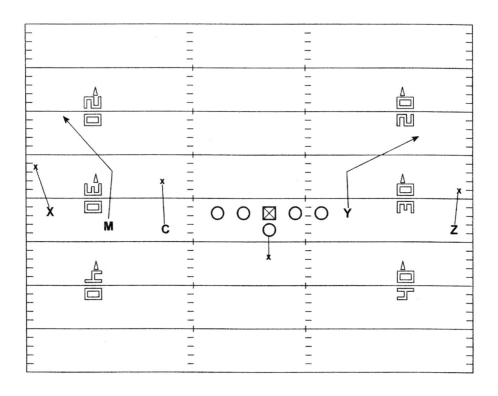

O-Line	Lion call
Y	Run a quick-corner route
Z	Run a smash route
X	Run a smash route
C	Run a smash route
M	Run a quick-corner route
QB	Take a 3-step drop

Play #101—Trey Right Spread 49

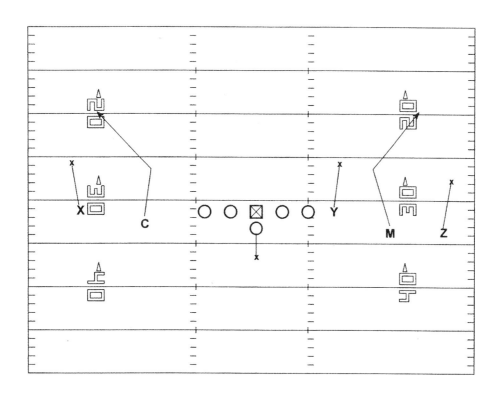

O-Line	Ram call
Y	Run a smash route
Z	Run a smash route
X	Run a smash route
TB	Run a quick-corner route
FB	Run a quick-corner route
QB	Take a 3-step drop

About the Authors

Stan Zweifel is the offensive coordinator and wide receivers/quarterbacks coach at the University of Wisconsin-Whitewater, a position he has held since 1990. During his tenure on the Warhawks staff, the team has achieved national recognition for its offensive prowess. Consistently, his offense has been nationally ranked in total offense, scoring offense, and rushing offense.

Prior to joining the coaching staff at the University of Wisconsin-Whitewater in 1992, Zweifel was the head football coach at the University of Minnesota-Morris, where his team won the 1987 NIC Championship and compiled a 22-18 record during his four-year tenure. He has also served as the offensive coordinator at the University of Northern Colorado, as the offensive coordinator at Mankata State University in Minnesota, and as the head football coach at Yankton College. Zweifel began his coaching career as a high school head football coach in New Ulm, Minnesota, where he coached for four years.

During his coaching career, Zweifel has produced more than a dozen All-American players, as well as numerous All-Region and All-Conference players. He has also seen several of his players go on to play professional football. This past year, he was named the Wisconsin College Assistant Coach of the Year by the Wisconsin Football Coaches Association.

Zweifel is an accomplished speaker who has spoken at numerous football clinics across the United States. He has authored or co-authored several best-selling instructional coaching books, including *Coaching Football's Zone Offense*, which is currently in its second edition. He is widely regarded nationally as one of the game's foremost experts on the zone blocking concept in football. He has also been featured on a number of well-received instructional videos and DVDs.

He and his wife, Diane, have four children—daughters, Saree and Shannon, and sons, Michael and Mark.

Robert Leboeuf is the head football coach at Whitnal High School in Milwaukee, Wisconsin, a position he assumed in 2004. Prior to that, he spent five seasons as an assistant football coach at Muskego (WI) High School—the first two as a position coach and the final three as the offensive coordinator. His efforts on the Muskego staff helped the Warriors establish a multiple-formation, clock-managing zone offense. In the process, his Muskego teams set several school records for total yardage and made the playoffs three times.